People of the Trail

FIREFLY BOOKS

People of the Trail

How the Northern Forest Indians Lived

Robin & Jillian Ridington
Illustrations by Ian Bateson

A Firefly Book

To our children: Karolle and Diana, who
know the animals and the forests; Mykaljon
and Aballi, who love a good story; Amber
and Juniper, with hope that they too will
come to care for these things.

Copyright © Robin Ridington and Jillian Ridington, 1978
Illustrations copyright © Ian Bateson, 1978
First published in Canada by:
Douglas & McIntyre

This edition published in the
United States in 1995 by:

Firefly Books (U.S.) Inc.
P.O. Box 1325
Ellicott Station
Buffalo, N.Y.
14205

Cataloguing in Publication Data

Ridington, Robin, 1939-
   People of the trail
  (How they lived in Canada)

ISBN 0-88894-412-8 (pbk.)

1. Indians of North America — Canada —
Juvenile literature. I. Ridington, Jillian,
1936-   II. Title III. Series.

E78.C2R53   j971'.004'97   C78-002161-4

Typesetting by Frebo Studio Limited
Book design by Ian Bateson
Cover design by Karen Harris
Printed and bound in Canada by
D.W. Friesen & Sons Ltd.

Contents

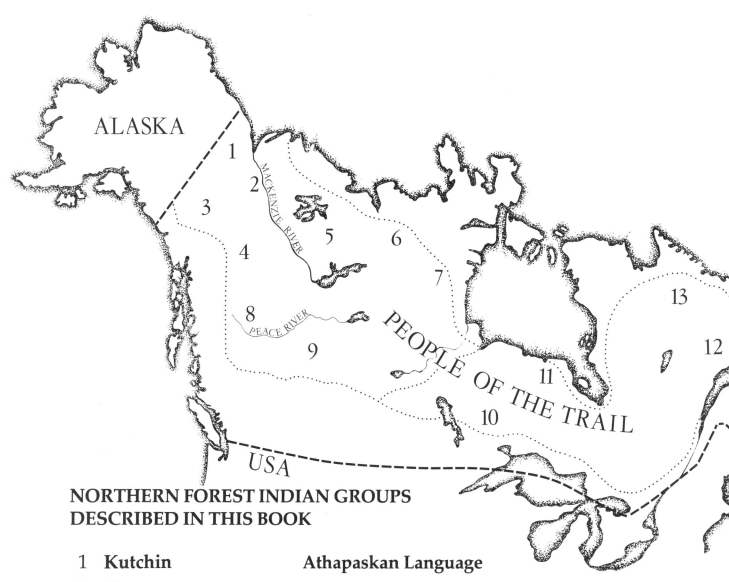

ALASKA

1

2 MACKENZIE RIVER

3

4

5

6

7

8 PEACE RIVER

9

PEOPLE OF THE TRAIL

13

12

11

10

USA

NORTHERN FOREST INDIAN GROUPS
DESCRIBED IN THIS BOOK

1	**Kutchin**	**Athapaskan Language**
2	**Hare**	
3	**Tutchone**	
4	**Kaska**	
5	**Dogrib**	
6	**Yellowknife**	
7	**Chipewyan**	
8	**Sekani**	
9	**Beaver**	
10	**Cree**	**Algonkian Language**
11	**Northern Ojibwa**	
12	**Montagnais**	
13	**Naskapi**	

The Land

The Indians of the northern part of North America, like all Indians, lived close to the land. They used everything the land offered for food, clothing and shelter — the three things that people everywhere must have. They would have been cold, hungry, sick or lost if they had not understood and respected their land and its animals.

The northern forest extends from Labrador to the Rocky Mountains, then north to Alaska. To the south lie the Great Plains and to the north the treeless arctic barrens. In the east the land is flat, dotted with lakes and laced with rivers. In the west, hills roll towards the Rocky Mountains.

It is a land of extreme contrasts, seemingly two different lands in summer and in winter. The short summer is a season of sunlight and flowing water, of flowers and foliage, of geese, ducks and songbirds, of beavers building dams and lodges and gathering sticks for winter food. The brilliant rose purple fireweed brightens open areas that have been cleared by recent forest fires. Dwarf alder and willow fill the older clearings, providing food for moose. Bears forage for berries and grubs and browse on juicy grasses and wild celery, storing fat for the long winter sleep. Mosquitoes and blackflies swarm in thick clouds out of the muskeg, the wet, mossy soil spiked with jackpines which is their breeding ground. Frogs sing in every body of water. The sun barely dips below the horizon; twilight comes at midnight. With the sun shining so long each day, the land becomes very hot; temperatures of 42° C are common in July and August.

The winter is long, with snow as early as September and as late as May. December to March are the coldest months, when sometimes the temperature is as low as −43° C. Geese, ducks and songbirds have followed the sun's warmth south; beaver lodges are frozen into ice and blanketed in snow; bears, mosquitoes, blackflies and frogs sleep away the winter. The sun is low in the southern sky and appears for only a few hours a day. The land is white, black and grey. The poplars, willows, dwarf alder, larches, cottonwoods and birches have lost their leaves; only the green of the stately spruce and the small pine, and an occasional wind blowing warm from the south, remind the people that the earth will become warm again.

The people of the northern forest cannot follow the sun south like the geese, hibernate like the bears, grow thick winter hair like the moose, or eat bark and grass and moss. They must stay and make the cold winter land their home. Since they live most of the year entirely on meat and fish, they follow the animals from one range to another. They are the people of the trail: their lives and the life of the land are one. If the animals come together in large numbers for a time, the Indians also come together in large numbers; when the animals split into smaller groups, the Indians too split into smaller groups.

For the northern nomads, early spring is the hardest time, for their stored food is running out and the bounty of the summer is still months away. The breaking up of the ice makes fishing unsafe. The fat stored under the skin of bears is gone and they, like

the people, are hungry. Berries will not ripen for months.

The first spring foods will be the inner bark of the poplar, sweet and fresh when the sap begins to flow, and the beavers and muskrats that can swim in open water when the ice breaks up.

In contrast, fall is a time of colour and plenty. The land is golden and scarlet with the turning leaves of poplars, birches and drying grass. Fat moose and caribou can be hunted; saskatoonberries, which ripen after the raspberries, blueberries and huckleberries of midsummer, can be dried and stored. Spring is a time of waiting, autumn a time of preparation.

Chipewyan Indian hunter on the trail

The People

The people of the trail are not short and stocky like the Inuit, their height and weight being about the same as ours. Before the coming of the white people, both men and women wore their hair long, often tied behind their necks with a leather thong. They spoke many different languages; those who lived east of Hudson Bay spoke Algonkian languages such as Naskapi, Northern Ojibwa and Cree; those to the west spoke Athapaskan languages, which included Chipewyan, Slavey and Beaver. Each group of languages came from a common root but so long ago that they had become quite different; Indians from one group could not easily understand those from the other, just as people who speak only English do not understand German, although the two languages are of the same family. Having no written language, they could not communicate by writing letters. When they wanted to meet with someone they left signs such as blazes — cuts made through the bark of trees to bare the wood beneath. These signs told the people when it was time to come together, and where to meet.

Indians are classified into tribes whose separate areas can be shown on maps like the one at the beginning of this book, but they did not think of themselves as being divided in that way. They felt close to those who spoke the same language.

They did not live in permanent villages and so did not have many possessions. They did not erect totem poles or carve objects from stone or bone simply to own beautiful things. But they did not

Dogrib band

Algonkian style cradle

think of themselves as poor just because they had few possessions. Being nomadic, they did not want many things to carry. They were rich in knowledge of their forest home and in stories about their people and the animals they knew so well.

They travelled and hunted in bands of 25 to 35 people who were related to each other by blood or marriage. Although everyone knew how they were related to the others in the band, their names for each other were not so limited in meaning as names in English. Sisters and female cousins might be called by the same term, and aunts and uncles referred to as Mother and Father. This practice helped children to understand that there were many adults who could teach and protect them.

Each band had its leaders, and the man who was the most skilled hunter was held in high regard, but there were no formal chiefs until the white men appointed them in order to make trading easier.

There were no large wars, but feuding occurred. Occasionally, men of one band would raid a camp of a traditional enemy — perhaps because their hunting ground had been invaded. Men might be killed and women taken as captive wives, but no one was made a slave to be sold or killed at an owner's will, and no scalps were taken. Because war was not very important in their lives, the forest people had no shields or armour.

Men are least likely to feud with those most like themselves, so raids occurred most often where territories bordered those of Inuit or Northwest Coast people.

The Family

Algonkian puberty drinking tube

Both boys and girls married young, having learned how to support themselves by watching and helping their elders throughout their childhood; they did not need years of schooling to earn their living.

When a young girl had her first menstruation, she was able to have babies, and was prepared for marriage. She was secluded in a hut away from the camp and was visited only by an older woman who taught her how to be a good wife. She wore special clothing, ate special food, and ate and drank from special utensils that might include a drinking tube made from the leg bone of a swan. Because the girl was in a time of transformation, changing from a girl into a woman, she was considered very powerful. Swans were associated with transformations, for they were powerful birds who could fly to other worlds and return. They followed trails to the heavens, just as the people followed trails on earth. For this reason, swans, and their feathers, down and bones, are still often found in the myths and rituals of the trail people.

For a boy, the first kill of game was very important. No matter how small it was, it was cooked and shared among the people of the camp. Each time the boy caught a new kind of animal, the same ceremony occurred. When he had proven himself as a provider of meat, he was ready for marriage.

Among some bands, marriage customs were quite different from our own. Most bands had no formal ceremony; a man and woman just began living together and referring to each other as husband and wife. The arrival of the first child confirmed the marriage. A young girl might marry an older, experienced hunter who would provide well for her and the babies she would have. A young boy might marry an older woman whose children were less dependent, so that the woman could help with fishing and trapping. It was possible to have more than one spouse, and if a sister of a wife were widowed, or a husband's brother left a widower, they might be taken as a second spouse so that they could be looked after. Since it was difficult to survive without a partner, almost everyone was married, although occasionally people would stop living together and find other partners. Work was divided: women dressed the hides, made clothes, gathered firewood, caught small game animals with their own snares, fished, and cooked; men hunted game, fished, and made hunting equipment, snowshoes, toboggans and canoes. Because young women had many children and nursed their infants for several years, they could not leave camp for long periods of time, so only older women hunted large game for themselves.

A woman gave birth by herself, or was helped by her husband or a midwife, and was secluded away from the main camp. After her child was born, it was wrapped in soft moss and skin and placed in a basket or in a pouch which the mother could carry on her back. Part of the child's umbilicus was put in a

Shaman's rattle (Algonkian)

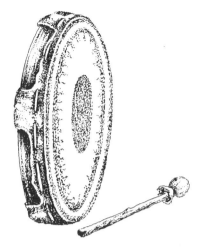

Drum

small skin bag which was attached to the baby's clothing to ward off evil spirits. The life of the trail people was often hard, and required the people to be strong and healthy. Babies, most susceptible to illness and least able to bear cold, often died. Because of this, babies were not named until it seemed that they were strong and would live.

Plants provided medicine that cured many illnesses. The pitch and needles of pine and the new tips of spruce gave infusions (teas) and poultices for cold, flu, insect bites, and wounds. Many other plants were dried to use in treating diseases.

Illness, like death, was believed to be caused by evil spirits or by enemies using supernatural power. A shaman, a kind of doctor, tried to find the cause of an illness and remove it by various methods. Montagnais-Naskapi and Cree shamans would have a special tent built in the shape of a cylinder or of a dome. Entering it, they would call their spirit helpers by singing and drumming. These spirit helpers were believed to come and go through the top of the tent, causing the tent to shake. Speaking through the shaman, they would give the cause and the cure for a patient's illness. Shamans were also believed to share the swan's ability to go to other worlds and return, and they would use ceremonies like the "shaking tent" ceremony to learn the future, or the whereabouts of distant people or animals. All shamans would treat sick people by removing the object which the power of the enemy had placed within the patient, or by returning the patient's lost soul.

Shaman singing over a patient

Although many infants and children died, some people lived to be very old. When in 1977 a Beaver Indian woman died, she was reported to have been 116, the oldest woman in Canada. Death other than death from very old age was thought to happen because bad spirits had entered the body, or because the person had done something evil. The evil spirits were believed to endanger the living, so dead bodies were taken away from the camp and placed high in trees, covered with logs at the base of a tree, or burned. Today, they are buried, and small wooden grave houses are built above the graves.

Games

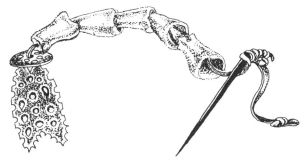

Cup and pin game

Sports and games train people in the skills they need to be successful in their culture. People who get their livelihood from the forest need to be able to judge distances, pick up clues and signs from the world around them, and conceal their presence in order not to disturb animals

Among the games played by the early boreal forest people was one in which men threw axes, aiming at the last thrower's weapon which might be embedded in a tree trunk or in the ground. In one very old game, a bone ring was tossed into the air and the thrower tried to spear it onto a pin which he held in his hand. These games improved the players' accuracy and helped them judge distances.

Boys played with bows and arrows and tried to pitch objects closest to a line or into a circle. In a wintertime game of accuracy called snow snake, a long thin stick was thrown under the snow.

Some men's games were guessing games. One team would conceal an object and the other team would have to guess where the object was. The guesser had to be very observant and his opponents very careful not to accidentally give any clues to the hiding place. These games were called "moccasin games" by the men of the eastern forest and "hand games" by those of the west.

Among the Dogrib and other Northern Athapaskans a very complex kind of hand game was
played. In the long nights of summer, teams of men
competed with men from different regions or bands.
Each member of one team concealed a token in his
hand. The other team chose a "guesser," who used a
complicated set of hand signals to guess the
placement of the tokens in each opponent's hand.
The hand game was played very quickly. The hiding
team squatted in front of drummers, and the noise
of the drumming and chanting added to the
excitement of the game. The motions of the players
as they swayed to the music made it harder for the
guesser to see what their hands were doing.

Both the players and the drummers bet on the
game. The score was kept with sticks and pegs. Each
player who concealed his token successfully was
given a stick; those who did not were "dead" and
had to drop out of the game. When all the men of
one team were dead, the drums and sticks were
passed to the opposing team and a new round
began. The game was often played for hours while
the rest of the men of the camp looked on.

Some games, such as the Chipewyan "bowl and
dice" game, played with flat pieces of bone, wood,
or stone whose sides were of different colours or
shapes, the lacrosse-like "double-ball" game of
some Algonkians, and the cup and pin game were
also played by girls and women, but most games
were played only by boys and men, who had more
leisure because their work was done only at certain
seasons.

Girls were sometimes given dolls carved from

wood and pieces of hide with which to sew small garments.

Games such as snow snake and the hand game are still played today.

Hand game

Hunting & Fishing

The rocky land of the northern forest has never been suitable for farming, and even the wild plants that grow there do not provide much food except for berries, which are plentiful in the summer and can be dried for winter use.

Without fish and game the early Indians would have starved. Because their lives were so dependent on all the animals they hunted, they felt a strong relationship towards their prey, which met in the same areas and at the same time each year, just as different bands met regularly.

Their most important game, moose and caribou, move in different ways. Moose usually live and travel by themselves, only occasionally meeting each other. Caribou migrate in herds, covering a large territory each season. Hunters followed the moose from one range to another, but when hunting caribou they would wait for them at a good hunting spot along the caribou's seasonal trails.

Whitefish and jackfish were caught in lakes, and arctic grayling and trout in rivers. Weirs, nets, traps or hooks were used, or the fish were speared. They were caught from the shore or from canoes in summer, and through holes cut in the ice in winter.

After the winter ice melted, traps were placed where beavers swam. When a beaver touched the centre pole of the trap, a door closed behind him.

Sometimes in winter a bear would be discovered in his den, and his meat would feed the camp for a few days. Rabbits were also eaten, as they are today, but their numbers vary widely in a seven-year cycle:

Fishing through the ice

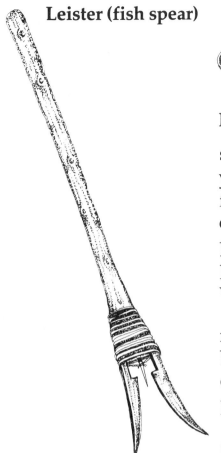

Leister (fish spear)

Slave Indian fish hook

Kaska fish hook

some years there are rabbits everywhere; other years, there are almost none. The smaller fur-bearing animals, mink and wolverine for example, were trapped in winter mainly for their pelts, but when other foods were unavailable, perhaps in late winter or early spring, these animals were also eaten.

When hunting was poor the people lived on dried meat and fish and on pemmican, a mixture of dried berries, dried meat and animal fat that was an excellent trail food because it provided vitamins and protein.

Land was not bought and sold in the way that it is today. A band was free to hunt and fish throughout a very large territory, but it would never go into an area if it knew that another band was hunting there. Knowing that their lives depended on game, the band members moved often so that they did not take too many animals from one area. They always left enough animals to breed so that there would be game in years to come.

When the bands that had come together during the summer found that the hunters were not bringing in enough meat to feed every family, they knew that it was time for each band to separate and hunt in different areas.

Because they had to travel by foot or by canoe the people moved their camp small distances of 32 to 48 km fairly often instead of making long

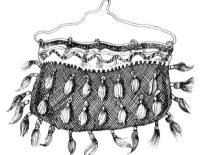

Small game hunting bag made of netted babiche

Ice scoop used for winter fishing

Beaver trap

hunting trips from their camp each day.

They studied the animals carefully and kept count of their numbers in each area. They did not think that hunting depended on luck but on skill and accurate information. They knew as much about the habits, life cycle, and location of the animals they hunted as farmers know about the animals they raise. When a hunter found an animal and killed it, he did not think that he had been simply "lucky," and when a hunter came home empty-handed after he had tried many times his people did not say that he was just "unlucky," but that he had been greedy or careless, or that he was hunting in an area after he should have moved away.

The hunters shared with each other all that they knew about an area and its game so that each hunter could decide where to hunt and the whole band could decide when and where to move. Like farmers who change crops so as to preserve the soil, the northern nomads changed their hunting grounds to preserve the game.

A hunter might travel alone, trapping with snares or killing with spears or bows and arrows. Men would also hunt together to surround an animal from different directions or to chase a herd into a

Deadfall trap

**Double snowshoe
bird trap**

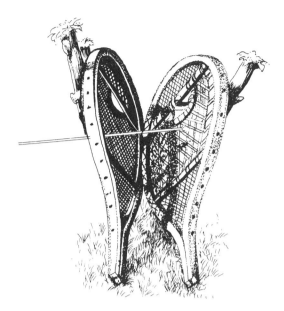

place where they could easily be killed. Sometimes a fence to trap caribou or moose was built. Other traps, used by women as well as men, caught birds and smaller game.

When hunters returned to camp with meat, they shared it with everyone in the band. It was unthinkable that one family would eat while others went hungry. Everyone knew that if he shared his food, in turn he would receive meat when his own hunting was unsuccessful. Small bands were the best because the meat of a single animal could feed all their members for a longer time than if the band were very large.

The places where hunting was good changed from time to time. Caribou sometimes changed their migration routes and the people had to move to where the caribou would be found. Moose live best in areas where there have been forest fires, for then their preferred food of alder and willow will grow in place of pine and spruce. From generation to generation, bands moved to where the moose were most abundant. Because the game population did not stay the same in every territory, the people had to move from one territory to another. This need for movement meant that although there were not many people, they required a large land area to live in.

Housing

With each move to a new location, a band would set up camp in a similar pattern. The rising sun symbolized the trail that lay ahead and its touch brought good fortune in the future; therefore each dwelling's entryway and sleeping places were arranged so that the early morning rays touched the faces of the people. The layout of the camp varied from band to band, but the relationship to the rising sun was always the same.

Winter ridgepole lodge

Shelters were made from the building materials available in each new campsite, so a home would not always be an exact copy of the family's last one, for the trees were different in different parts of the forest. Summer houses did not need to be as sturdy as winter houses. The people had to erect shelters quickly when a new camping ground was reached, and because they had no hammers, nails or saws, they used only small trees, which they cut down with stone axes. For one type of winter house, poles were laid close together with the narrow ends at the top to form a tepee shape, then the chinks between the poles were filled with earth or moss. Summer houses could be made of animal skins stretched over pole frames and laced together with babiche,

Summer birch lodge

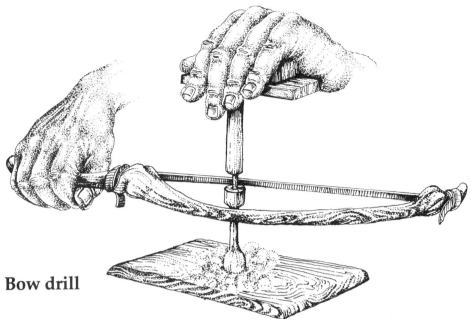

Bow drill

the long strips of rawhide which the people used as rope. In the east, strong birch bark was used for summer lodges.

There were many different styles of houses built, most being quite small, 3.5 to 4.5 m across. Some were shaped like domes, others like conical tents or tepees of the Plains Indians, and some like ridgepole tents. Among the Athapaskans, a "double lean-to" shelter was used during the summer.

When it was time for a celebration or a ceremony, a larger dance hut was built. It was made to the same tepee design as smaller houses, but twice as big so that the entire band could gather inside it. Each family contributed skins and worked to help make the dance lodge. When it was finished the women and small children, the hunters, the old people, the older boys and girls all sat in groups in their own special sections of the lodge. The fire was built in the middle and the people danced and sang around it, a few at a time.

Although there were many different kinds of houses, one feature was always the same: the centre of each house was the fire. The people carried their fire from camp to camp, using burning sticks to light the trail. If the flames went out, a new fire was started with a bow drill or by striking flint on pyrite (an iron ore containing sulpher) in a bed of partially

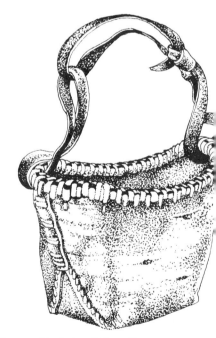

Dogrib birchbark water ve and drinking cup

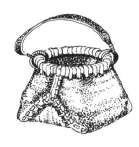

Family life in camp

rotted dry wood. Fire was used for cooking, heat and light. Food was either roasted on sticks over the open fire or boiled in birch bark baskets hung from a tripod. Stones from the open fire were lifted with tongs and placed in the food basket to make the liquid boil.

In the winter the fire warmed a circle in which the old people could sit while they told stories of the history and ways of their people. In the spring and summer the smoke from the fires helped keep mosquitoes and blackflies away.

Fire was the focus of family life. In fact, in the Beaver Indian language the words meaning camp, home and fire all come from the same root word, so that when one word is spoken the others come immediately to mind.

Clothing

The northern forest Indians had no sheep to provide wool, so their clothing was made from the skins of animals. Sewing and decorating were just the final steps in a long process that began with skinning the animal and carefully scraping, smoking and working the hide until it was soft and supple. Then it was cut with a knife into shapes that would become moccasins, a woman's dress or leggings, a

Hide working

man's shirt or jacket, or a small child's snowsuit. Because no metal was available for sharp needles a bone awl was used to make holes through which to pull the sinew.

All members of the family wore moccasins throughout the year. This supple footwear gave the

Awl and hide scraper

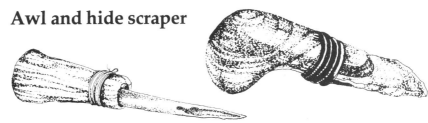

feeling of going barefoot but kept the feet warm and protected during even the coldest weather. For people of the trail good footwear was very important, as were the mitts or gauntlets, also made of animal hide, which protected their hands from cold.

They did not need heavy clothing to keep them warm as the Inuit did, for they relied on their campfires for warmth when they were not on the

Kutchin hunter

Yellowknife Indian summer costume

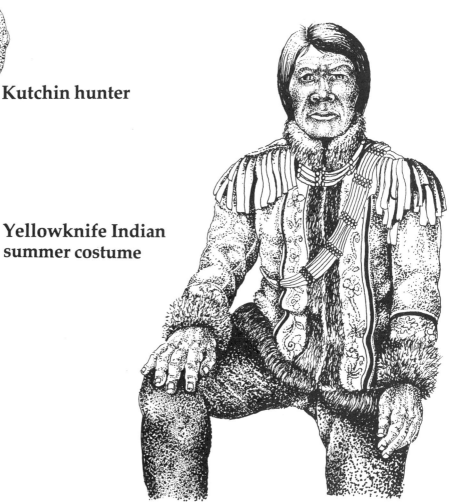

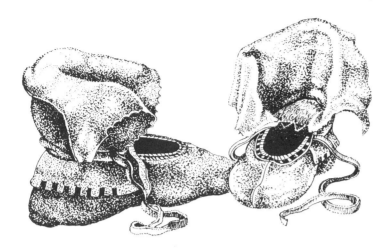

Dogrib moccasins

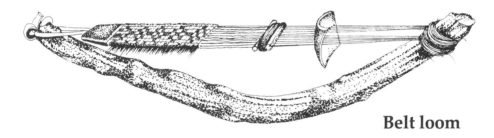

Belt loom

move. No forest Indian wore a hood unless he was one of a band that lived close to the Inuit and copied their clothing style. The Indians' clothing was warm and serviceable but light enough to allow them to move freely and quickly.

The women spent long hours decorating clothing with lovely designs made from porcupine quills and moosehair, and some garments were as beautiful as the pictures in any art gallery. After trading with white people began, needles, silk embroidery thread, beads and felt cloth came into use and the designs became even more elaborate.

Fur was used for hats, for socks to wear inside moccasins in winter, and for mitt liners. Robes for sleeping and for wrapping up small children were made from rabbit skins cut into thin strips which were first twisted, then woven together.

On the Trail

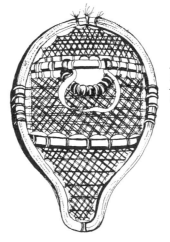

Long snowshoes (left) and beavertail snowshoes

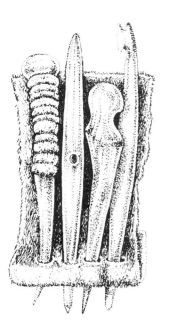

Tool kit for lacing snowshoes

Most northern Indians travelled on foot. Because of the deep winter snow they developed snowshoes which enabled them to walk on the surface of the snow rather than sink down into it. Snowshoes were of different designs for different snow conditions and different terrain, but some of the differences were simply a matter of style. In the west the common style was long and thin; in the east, rounded. Some groups used dog teams pulling toboggans for speed and to help carry food, supplies, and people too old or sick to walk. In areas where food was usually too scarce to feed a team of dogs throughout the year, toboggans might be pulled by women and children and pushed by men or pulled by a woman while the man broke trail ahead. Because sled runners sink into deep snow, sleds were used less often than toboggans and only where there was hard-packed snow or ice.

In the summertime people on the trail put packs on their dogs. The pack on a traveller's back was supported by a tumpline around his or her forehead. A baby would be carried on its mother's back in a specially made carrier of birch bark and hide.

Family on the winter trail

Wherever possible, canoes were used to carry loads in the summer. They were particularly useful in the eastern forest, where rivers and lakes linked to form a network of waterways. Made from the bark of birch trees, they were much lighter and smaller than the cedar canoes of the Northwest Coast. Being light, they could be carried or "portaged" across the land between bodies of water. The use of canoes enabled the northern forest people to travel swiftly and far.

Before leaving a campsite a group would often place extra tools and food in a storage place called a cache, which was built on a platform or in a tree or occasionally dug in the ground. They could then be sure of tools and food when they came back to the same place, and would not have to carry unnecessary weight on the trail.

The Indians had to be able to find their way over many kilometres of dense bush. By paying careful attention to the sun's position in its path across the sky each day, they could tell which direction to travel to return safely to camp. They also watched the sun's passage to the north in the summer and to the south in the winter, for it marked changes in the life of the land brought on by the change of season. Their stories told of the sun flying north and south like the geese and ducks; their dances circled around the fire, following the direction that the sun seems to follow in its path around the world. They believed that throughout their lives people circled around the world and came back to the place where their relatives were camped, just as the sun circles around the world and comes back in the eastern sky.

Because their lives were tied so closely to their

Portaging

land, to the animals, and to the seasons, they were
very careful to behave in ways that would not
change the natural order of things. They believed
that if they slept with their heads to the east they
would dream about the trail that lay ahead of them,
and in their dreams the animals would give their
bodies to the hunters who had respected them, who
had been careful not to overhunt, and who had
shared their meat with everyone in their camp.
When they went hunting they followed the
directions given to them in their dreams, using the
sun's position in the sky as their guide.

Dreams were very important and very real. In
dreams their minds brought together everything
they knew about hunting and gave them a picture of
the best place to hunt and the best path to follow.
The people of the trail studied their dreams as we
study maps when planning a trip. They trained
themselves to dream intelligently, and before going
to sleep they would think about what they knew
about the game animals from the traditional stories,
from their own experience, and from the shared
experiences of older hunters. They had trained
themselves to remember everything they saw and
everything that happened to them, so that in their
dreams they could draw upon the information
stored in their minds, just as we draw information
from books stored in libraries. Because his dreams
were based on the best information available to him,
and because the dreams were very real to him, a
hunter on the trail would not get tired or
discouraged easily but would keep on until he found
and caught his prey.

Beliefs & Education

The beliefs, stories and ceremonies of the people of the northern forest show how their lives were closely tied to the lives of the animals. All living things — rivers, plants, the earth itself as well as people and animals — were believed to have spirits which must be respected. One way that children learned to understand and respect their relationship to animals and to the other people in the band was through the vision quest that they went on just before they reached puberty.

In preparation for their vision quest, they were told stories of a time when giant animals hunted people, and of the hero who rescued his people by turning the hunters into the hunted. After that time, animals gave their lives so that the people could live. The hero taught the people how to track and capture animals and how to use them for food and clothing. Never again did the people have to go hungry or cold.

Each boy or girl had to go alone into the forest and stay there until he or she met a special friend or protector in the form of an animal. On returning to camp the child would bring back the power of that special animal and the wisdom of the hero of the stories. With this power and knowledge a new generation of men became able in dreams to get in touch with the animals that they would hunt, and a new generation of women learned the sensitivity to be worthy makers of food and clothing from these animals. The people of the trail did not use any form of writing; for them, reading consisted of scanning the land for signs of animals or the trails of their people and making sense of these

Dreamer

First geese of the year killed

signs. The vision quest helped them to develop this ability.

Each tribe had ceremonies to hold when the men were to leave on a long hunt. In Labrador, the Naskapi Indians threw bones into the fire, believing that wise people could tell from the cracks in the bones which trails should be followed to find animals and food. The result of this ceremony was a plan of the area to be hunted, which they could use in a way similar to the way we use maps. This ritual was called "scapulomancy."

The shamans, or dreamers, who cured the sick also advised the people and conducted the rituals that took place at times of birth, death, or during other significant events in their lives; when changes in the weather were needed; and to ensure the return of game and of the growing season.

Like the plains people to the south of them, the Indians had drums with which to make music when they danced and sang. The rhythm of their drums was steady and regular, something like the beating of a heart. Music and dancing were especially important, for the people believed that drums, like dreams, could reveal the trail to follow. When a person died, the beating of the drums and the movement of the tune showed his spirit the way to heaven. If a person had been selfish or cruel during the time he was alive, it was believed that his spirit would be heavy and so have a hard time going up to heaven. Dancing while you were alive lightened your spirit so that it could float up to heaven when it left your body.

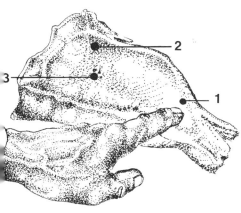

1 **Location of camp**

2 **Caribou**

3 **Indicates location
   and number of Indians
   and possibility
   that they have meat**

The ceremonies, like the stories told by the old people, taught children their history and their world. The children did not just enjoy stories, as we enjoy "fairy tales"; to them, stories and experience were all one. The sun that give them direction was the hero of their stories; he had come to earth to transform things and make things good for the people, then watched them from the sky to see them live in the way he had made possible. The stories, ceremonies and rituals made it easier for children to learn and understand their place among their people and in their world.

The children also learned the skills that would enable them to survive as adults. There were no classrooms, but they had to learn to paddle a canoe, snowshoe, read the tracks of animals, know the trails, streams, trees and plants in an area of many thousand square kilometres, process hides and food, and make clothing, traps and utensils. The tools they used were simple and made from stone, wood or bone, but their very simplicity meant that great skill was needed to use them well. And knowing how to make a snare out of strips of animal hide was only the beginning; the use of that snare required an understanding of the habits of animals that had been taught to young hunters for hundreds of years. Similarly, great skill went into making the light, supple and warm clothing needed to protect the people on the trail. Gradually throughout their childhood, girls learned this skill by watching as adult women made garments using only hides, sinew and simple awls and scrapers.

38

The children of the trail were never physically punished for behaving badly but rather learned if the things they did were good or bad by the reaction of other people. Ridicule, gossip and scolding were the most effective means of controlling the behaviour of children — and adults too. In the band, where everyone's life depended on sharing with others, no one could afford to risk disgrace and ill will, so considerate behaviour was soon learned.

When the white men came, the Indian children had to go to schools run by missionaries, and these schools were sometimes far away from their families, so they could go home only for the summer holidays or at Christmas. They were taught in English and forbidden to speak their native language. The unfortunate result of this kind of schooling was that the children did not learn how to cook, hunt or make clothes in traditional ways and that passages to maturity were not observed with the proper ceremonies. Then they could not communicate as well with their people.

Efforts are now being made to teach native languages and skills as well as the reading, science and mathematics that the children need today if they want to live in the world of white people.

Spirit passing to heaven in death ceremony

Coming of the White People

The people of the northern forest were both the first and the last native North Americans to meet people whose customs and values were very different from their own. The Montagnais of Labrador probably traded furs to Breton fishermen as long ago as 1500 AD, but the northern people, who were a long way from water and so out of easy reach by explorers and traders, did not have regular contact with white people until about 150 years ago.

The fur trade brought them steel tools, blankets, guns that made hunting far easier, and beads to decorate their clothing more quickly and brightly. But the coming of the white people also brought diseases such as smallpox and tuberculosis which killed a great many Indians who had no resistance to diseases that were new to this continent.

The white men also brought different ideas that caused conflict. Because the Indians did not believe in the white people's God and did not think that land should be sold by individuals or bands, the white people and the Indians often misunderstood each other. As the whites moved into the land where the Indians hunted and had travelled freely, disagreements arose over how the land should be used and who had the right to be there. White people did not understand that the Indians needed large areas in which to hunt; they thought that the land was not being used because no farms or permanent houses were on it.

Many Indians signed treaties with white people, giving up the rights to certain areas where they had lived in return for other pieces of land; these lands were known as reserves because they were reserved for the use of native people. Some native people now feel that the treaties were not fair because the Indian people who signed them did not really understand the meaning of the words. In some parts of the northern forest no treaties were signed, and the Indians claim that the land is their land.

The northern forest was once useful to the white man only for the furs he could get from the Indians through trade, but now this land is valuable because of oil, gas, minerals and the electrical energy that can be generated from the rivers. All northern forest Indians continue to feel close to their land and see the land as a renewable resource that can continue to support future generations as it has supported their ancestors. Though they realize that their lives can never by the same as they were before the white people came, they want to make their living in the same way that their ancestors did – from the land and its animals. They do not want their land destroyed by white men searching for valuable resources.

The problem of native land claims must be solved, and the solutions must be fair to the people of the trail.